Accident Prone

Written by Quentin Flynn
Illustrated by Matt Golding

Contents	Page
Chapter 1. *The new neighbors*	4
Chapter 2. *Crash!*	10
Chapter 3. *Splash!*	16
Chapter 4. *Thump!*	24
Chapter 5. *Never-ending noise*	28
Verse	32

Rigby

Accident Prone

With these characters ...

Mrs. Fumblenoggin

Mr. Fumblenoggin

Dr. Doodleman

"I though

Setting the scene ...

It's a quiet Saturday on King Street. The moving van has arrived, and all the neighbors want to see who will be moving into the red house.

Dr. Doodleman is the most curious, as he lives next door. Soon, the new neighbors arrive to interrupt the peace and quiet of King Street, and Dr. Doodleman quickly finds out that these are no normal neighbors! If there are any disasters waiting to happen on King Street, they'll happen any minute now!

ey were moving in,
ot demolishing the house!"

Chapter 1.

King Street was a quiet street until the Saturday that the moving van parked outside the red house. The neighbors watched curiously as men started to unload boxes, furniture, and plastic bags from the truck.

No one was more curious than Dr. Doodleman. He lived next door, and he was always nosy. He decided to weed his front garden (even though there were no weeds), hoping to sneak a look at his new neighbors.

He didn't have to wait long. About five minutes later, a rusty old orange van swerved in behind the moving van. It was bursting with boxes, furniture, and plastic bags. Hunched behind the steering wheel was a tall, skinny man. Dr. Doodleman could just see one other head among the furniture and boxes inside the orange van.

CRASH! The little van hit the bumper of the moving van, and the boxes toppled off the roof all over the sidewalk. All the movers jumped to safety!

"Hello, hello!" waved the van driver cheerily, as he stepped out over the pile of boxes. "We're the Fumblenoggins. Pleased to meet you."

He stretched out to shake Dr. Doodleman's hand. He didn't notice one of the boxes in front of him.

THUMP! His glasses flew off as he tripped and slid into the wet grass by the sidewalk. Dr. Doodleman noticed that Mr. Fumblenoggin's glasses were held together by pieces of tape. Obviously, Mr. Fumblenoggin fell over a lot!

Mrs. Fumblenoggin tumbled out of the dented van, followed by more boxes. The neighbors waved politely at the Fumblenoggins.

Mr. Fumblenoggin struggled to stand up on the wet, slippery grass. As he picked up one of the boxes, it made strange clinking sounds.

"Sounds like broken cups and saucers," smiled Mr. Fumblenoggin, as he opened the gate with his foot. "Oh well, fewer dishes to wash!" He stumbled and staggered toward the door.

Mr. Fumblenoggin jumped up the steps. He whacked his forehead smack-dab on the top of the doorway. CRACK! Mrs. Fumblenoggin knew that sound. Her husband was just too tall, and he always forgot to bend down.

"I'm surprised that your forehead isn't as dented as our van," giggled Mrs. Fumblenoggin.

Dr. Doodleman rolled his eyes and went back inside his house, grumbling. Why couldn't he have a nice, quiet, normal family as neighbors?

Chapter 2.

Inside the red house, the Fumblenoggins unpacked their things.

"Just need some extra-strong glue," said Mr. Fumblenoggin brightly, as he looked at the broken cups and saucers in the box.

"Three legs are as good as four," said Mrs. Fumblenoggin cheerfully, as she looked at the broken chair in the middle of the living room.

"Not so far to fall if I roll off during the night," said Mr. Fumblenoggin happily, as he inspected the bed that had snapped in the middle.

The Fumblenoggins raced around the house, arranging and rearranging all their furniture. Even Dr. Doodleman could hear the loud crashing and thumping noises from next door.

"What *are* they doing?" he muttered, shaking his head as he tried to read his newspaper. "I thought they were moving in, not demolishing the house!"

"Let's take a break, Mr. Fumblenoggin," called out Mrs. Fumblenoggin from deep within the kitchen's pantry.

"Okey doke!" said Mr. Fumblenoggin, rushing in. He looked in a box and brought out a battered-looking teakettle.

Soon, the teakettle was boiling and bubbling. Mr. Fumblenoggin rubbed the bruise that the doorway had made on his forehead.

"Cups and saucers," he was muttering. He peered into the cardboard box that had the remains of the broken cups and saucers in it and rubbed his bruise again.

"I know what we can use!" he said, pointing at another box. "Plastic mugs! We'll have our hot cup of tea in plastic mugs."

He pulled out two plastic mugs and poured boiling water over a teabag in each one.

"Here we are, Mrs. Fumblenoggin," he said, as he picked up one of the mugs. There was a loud bump as Mrs. Fumblenoggin banged her head inside the pantry.

"Are you all right, Mrs. ... aah, aaah, AAAAH!"

Mr. Fumblenoggin's face turned bright red as the boiling hot plastic mugs started to melt in his fingers. He dropped the mugs, spilling the steaming hot tea on the floor.

"Oh well," said Mrs. Fumblenoggin, emerging from the pantry with a throbbing head. "The floor needed a good wash anyway."

Mr. Fumblenoggin was shaking his hands and shrieking as he rushed for the kitchen sink. He calmed down as the cold water soothed his burning hands. The Fumblenoggins mopped up the spilled tea and looked for their next job.

Chapter 3.

"Time to hang the paintings, Mr. Fumblenoggin," said Mrs. Fumblenoggin.

"Okey doke!" said Mr. Fumblenoggin, cheering up again. He found his hammer and picture hooks. Mrs. Fumblenoggin gathered up the paintings to hang in the hallway.

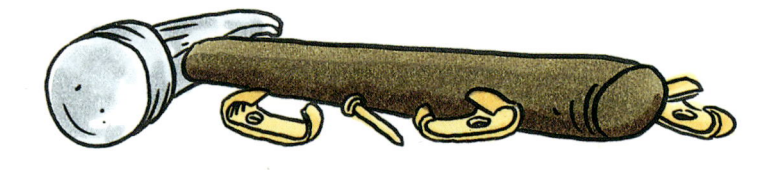

"How high?" asked Mr. Fumblenoggin. "This high?"

"Higher," said Mrs. Fumblenoggin.

"This high?" asked Mr. Fumblenoggin, placing the nail higher.

"Higher," said Mrs. Fumblenoggin.

Mr. Fumblenoggin put the nail higher.

"That's perfect!" said Mrs. Fumblenoggin.

Mr. Fumblenoggin pulled out his hammer from his pocket and took a huge, wobbly swing at the nail.

"OUCH!" he shouted, as he banged his thumb so hard it made a dent in the wall. He tried again, and the hammer went straight *through* the wall.

"At least you missed your thumb that time," said Mrs. Fumblenoggin.

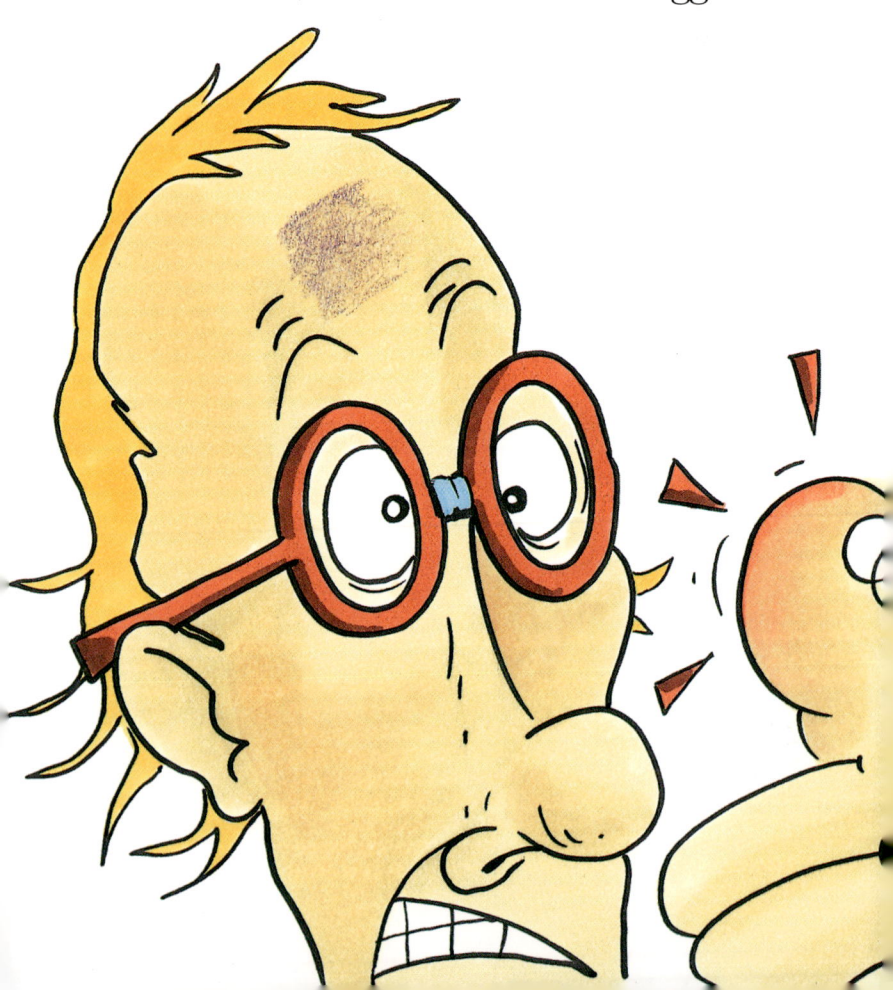

Mr. Fumblenoggin poked his finger into the hole.

"OUCH!" he yelled even louder, pulling his finger out of the hole at top speed. "I think there must be mighty big spiders in this house!" Both his finger and his thumb were throbbing with pain.

The Fumblenoggins were staring up at the hole when they noticed the white ceiling had some dirty marks on it.

"Time to do some painting, Mr. Fumblenoggin," said Mrs. Fumblenoggin.

"Okey doke!" said Mr. Fumblenoggin agreeably.

He came clanking down the hall, carrying his ladder, a can of paint, and a big paintbrush between his teeth. He stood on the first rung of the ladder, but he couldn't reach the ceiling. He stood on the second rung of his ladder but still couldn't reach the ceiling. He climbed to the very top of the ladder.

"Hold the ladder tight, Mrs. Fumblenoggin!" he called down. Drops of paint started to plop down onto Mrs. Fumblenoggin's head.

Mr. Fumblenoggin and his can of paint wobbled and wavered on top of the ladder.

Mr. Fumblenoggin finished painting the ceiling.

"How does that look?" he called down to Mrs. Fumblenoggin. Just as she looked up to see what it looked like, another drop of paint plopped down— right onto her glasses!

"I can't see a thing," she said, letting go of the ladder to wipe her glasses. Mr. Fumblenoggin started to wobble and waver even more than before. He leaned back to admire his work, which was exactly the *wrong* thing to do at that time.

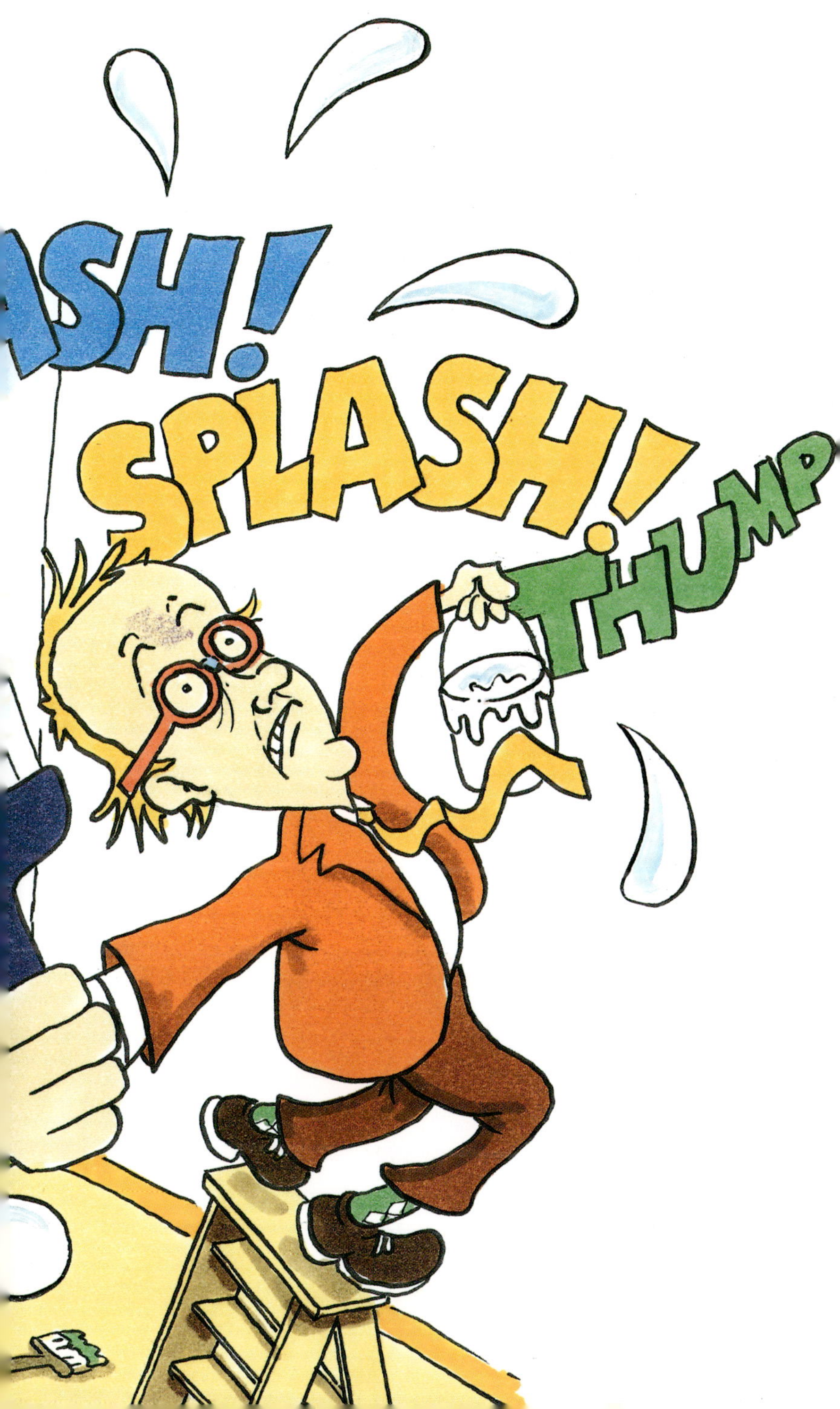

ASH!
SPLASH!
THUMP

Chapter 4.

"I never did like that carpet color," said Mr. Fumblenoggin, as he lay sprawled out in the paint puddle. Mrs. Fumblenoggin tried to agree, but all she could do was blow paint bubbles. Sloppy, big paint bubbles.

Suddenly, there was a loud knock at the door.

"Can you see who it is, Mr. Fumblenoggin?" gurgled Mrs. Fumblenoggin.

"Okey doke!" said Mr. Fumblenoggin. He squished along in his paint-soaked shoes and opened the door.

"Hello, Dr. Doodleman," he said cheerfully. He went to step out onto the porch but forgot about the doorway . . . again!

SMACK! A large, white paint stain the shape of Mr. Fumblenoggin's forehead appeared on the doorway.

Dr. Doodleman, who had come over to complain about all the noise, just stood and stared. He looked over Mr. Fumblenoggin's shoulder and saw a very wet, paint-covered Mrs. Fumblenoggin on the floor. He looked at Mr. Fumblenoggin's thumb, fingers, bruises, and burns.

"It's time to call the hospital," said Dr. Doodleman sternly.

"Okey doke!" gargled Mrs. Fumblenoggin, who stood up and slipped over *again* on the wet paint.

THUMP!

Chapter 5.

The Fumblenoggins were treated at the hospital. After they were cleaned up, their wounds were treated, covered in ointment, and bandaged.

Dr. Doodleman heard the doors of the orange van slam shut as they arrived home. He peeked through the window and quietly chuckled to himself.

"Now I've seen it all," he laughed. "Appendicitis. Tonsillitis. Laryngitis. And now . . . *Accidentitis!*"

Later that day, he was slowly drifting off into a nice peaceful doze, when he was suddenly woken up by a loud crash. He peeked out his window again.

"It's OK, Doc!" waved Mr. Fumblenoggin. He was standing on a wooden box by his front door.

"I'm just going to cut a hole in the top of this doorway. Don't want any more bumps on my forehead, *do* we? Where are my tools, Mrs. Fumblenoggin?"

Dr. Doodleman nodded and smiled. But when he saw what Mrs. Fumblenoggin brought to the door, he was *horrified*.

"No, no, no!" he shouted. But Mr. Fumblenoggin just grinned and started it up: a gigantic red CHAIN SAW!

"Oh, *no*," groaned Dr. Doodleman. "This will be *disastrous!*"

"Crash, Splash, Thump!"

Accidents
Foolish, frequent
Crashing and bashing
Just waiting to happen
Ouch!